THE BRIAR PATCH

THE
BRIAR PATCH

J. Kates

The Hobblebush Granite State Poetry Series, Volume V

HOBBLEBUSH BOOKS

Brookline, New Hampshire

Composed in Adobe Arno Pro at Hobblebush Books

Printed in the United States of America

Cover painting by Jane Pincus
Author photo by Helen Kates

ISBN: 978–0-9845921-8-0
Library of Congress Control Number: 2012938923

The Hobblebush Granite State Poetry Series, Volume V
Editors: Sidney Hall Jr. and Rodger Martin

HOBBLEBUSH BOOKS
17-A Old Milford Road
Brookline, New Hampshire 03033
www.hobblebush.com

Contents

Rule Number One: Everything's attached.
In the briar patch whichever way
you turn, somebody gets scratched.

Rule Number Two: Your eyes bleed
when they are plucked out and weep
when they are stuck in. Proceed

accordingly. Your oldest friend
needs that woman, that job no more
than you do. Friendships mend

if they are meant to. Have some fun.
Make some money. Get what you can.
Above all, look out for Number One.

HOW IT WAS

How It Was

In the beginning was the word,
and the word was without form and void.
Darkness played on the surfaces of water
while light gathered in the refractions of waves
like a congregation awaiting the hour of worship
or stars lining up into constellations.
Slowly the sun lifted itself over the horizon,
a vast red beast stirred by elements of hunger and love.
Behind it at a respectful distance jackalled a spotted moon
until evenings and mornings circled around each other
like a well-greased bicycle wheel that won't stop spinning.
Dry earth burgeoned and blossomed,
animals cautiously snouted out from thickets of metaphor
onto the vistas of savannah
and a predatory existence.
The clay shed sand to compose as Adam
who held everything in the palm of his tongue
and named the names of Creation.
Mock orange.
False Solomon's seal.

SIX-DAY WONDER

By the seventh day it was all over,
a thing to turn away from
and get some rest, as a kind of favor
for having created the humdrum.

Earth was a matter of fact. Flight,
creeping and swimming were other ways
of running around. The celebrated night-
and-day dichotomy had praise

from man, the delegate, whose chief end
was to make glory of all this
orderly chaos and pretend
that a small part of it was his.

The sun in place, nothing was new
under it. The stars were moved
because there was nothing else to do
but love, and be loved.

OPENING CHORUS

And through it all,
while we waited for the ship to arrive
with a black sail or a white sail,
while we made our own kind of love
in the morning and buried
our dead before nightfall,
the hair on our heads kept growing,
and our fingernails,
and without thinking
we cut them back, inch by inch,
and fell into bed again, or ditched
square holes in the lengthening shadow,
or stared unavailing at the silent horizon
while the hair on our heads kept growing
and our nails dug
into our hollow hands.

RANGE

The quivering of the arrow in the mark
and of the bowstring in the air
are simultaneous and identical
although removed in space, and where

the archer's hands were they remain unmoved.
The target shows that something changed,
the bow unbent reflects an alteration,
arrow and bow are not estranged—

archer and target shaft and field are brought
together by the letting go,
and what the bowstring whispered in my ear
at that one instant they all know.

IF ACHILLES WERE A POINT

Zeno would be king.

But Achilles was a warrior,
a man who ran
after a tortoise
to spoil it of its shell—
the raw material
of an eloquent
musical instrument,
an offering to his lover
on the anniversary
of their overtaking—

and who, as the distance
narrowed by halves,
plunged his arms forward
into the illogic of victory,

and Zeno
is a dead philosopher.

UNDERWATER

Underwater, under cold water
I pull and stroke, holding tight
to my chest the warm air,
letting it out in useless bubbles
by the count of kicks, farther
and farther from the shore.
Even here, there is above and below
darkening as I make for the center
of the wide lake, while overhead
a small circle of everyday
swims with me, always the same blue
and always ready to save my life.

GLACIER

The hand of God in the Sistine Chapel
is warm, life-giving with
only the suggestion of a touch. Supple
to wring out souls, or grapple
Jacob to the sacred myth.

The hand of God as I have seen it
in Athabaska is cold and stiff.
It holds the mountains between its
coarse fingers, squeezing just enough
to split the rough rock in its grip.

Here Michelangelo was nearly right—
it is in withdrawing the hand of God creates.
Rivers run from his fingers, lakes
spring from the heel of his palm-print,
and the free high horns gleam with a holy light.

DECEMBER THAW

A December thaw, like fabled April,
cracks open winter's white shell
until wet southern breezes ooze out,
messy and yellow in the evening sky.

And we, who are used to doing
what we are told by weather—
ski now—quick, run laundry up the rigging—
break wood, break wood, break wood—

caught at an embarrassing loss
and overdressed for the occasion
stick close to home
watching the stoves go cold,

knowing from news the way we know
elections, having lived long enough,
that tomorrow, like yesterday, will be winter,
and one day out of season is no gift.

CLOSE ENCOUNTER

"Universe Will Expand Forever"
—THE KEENE SENTINEL

Not from outer space, but from Vermont
or New Jersey, you drop in on us—
on your way down, say, from Toronto
or your way up to somewhere else.

You walk our woods, take copious notes
on the sound of birdsong, the look
of a crumbling sawmill, our domestic habits
and the exhalation of woodsmoke.

You are astonished how we live far
from the concrete lines that stitch your life,
you are dazzled when we meet the New Year
in a cosmopolitan flock of fifty—

Where do we all come from? you ask.
I put the same question to the deer
when I follow their unmistakable tracks
in new snow, although I never see them here.

Friend, the world is full of worlds. Every
point on earth and in the expanding sky
is a crossroads. Stars shed their silvery
light visibly all night—and all day.

ADVENT

for Matt and Barbara, and for Ben

Slow Sunday rain,
a water not worth walking out in,
steelpenny gray
grown over by the glittering
streetlights of a slaty night
too early among hours
for my slow Sunday taste.

Newspapers overripe with ads
rot like last month's pumpkins
on the stoop.
Nothing is coming,
it's already here:
skunks rummaging in the compost heap,
tomorrow's weather,

the jingling songs we're sick of,
not even a rough beast slouching
unless the wet cats
crying to be fed
or a special election
with no one special running.
Nothing is dry enough to burn.

We wait on the event
to make a season of these days:
a drop in temperature
crystallizing rain
to the snow it started out as,
the birth we have known about so long
that we had given up expecting.

The Genuine Monets

The genuine Monets,
the ones the painter painted
at Giverny,
are in museums
or other hands.

Scientific light
never wavers on the walls
where haystacks and Rouen
stare, each separate one,
at the changing people
who walk unsteadily and whisper on.

But I have a poster
of the pond with waterlilies
that I picked up at the Coop
for a dollar fifty.

And moving sunlight dances
every hour a different dance
around my waterlilies.
The shadow of the wooden bridge
alters with each cloud
outside my window.

Industrial Steel, Quai d'Orsay

There is something in me that turns to industrial steel
when I hear of stone Buddhas blown to savage rubble
or irreplaceable watercolors seared in a fire.
I care, but I do not grieve. All art is mortal.
And most of art honors mortality. Why should bronze
or gilded monuments or even these temperate words
outlive life? Life is its own tidal wave
and washes away whatever grows or is built—
sooner or later Venice and Ankgor Wat, the Spiral Jetty
and oh, this last Monet sketch of his dying wife
that makes me weep new tears every time I see it.

STARTING SCHOOL

On the opening day all you need
is a pencil in your fist.
If they can't give you a pencil
you've already learned the first lesson
and all you need is the fist.

THE DEAD

I would like to leave you to bury each other,
but you won't. You keep rising
out of the falling dust, refusing
to lie still long enough to smother.

You throw down in transparent disgust
the tools of your unwilling trade
and dice like strikers while the spade
and barrow blush in the creep of rust.

Everything's now at sixes and sevens,
long overdue for traditional rites;
striped awnings flap over your gravesites,
Hell gapes, and the overclouded heavens

threaten rain. We, your living,
demand fulfillment of this last
obligation. Lay one another to rest
and we will grieve. I will go on grieving.

IN INTERESTING TIMES

for Svetlana Bodrunova

The statue fell and shattered in the square.
Poets had trouble with that. Lacking a plinth
to plaster verses on, life wasn't fair.
We could rejoice in freedom for a month

or two, but liberation wore as thin
as the new flood of sleazy magazines
that showed nothing but skin, always more skin—
where was the blood? Where were the fucking bones?

The foreign press had other fish to fry.
Attention shifted to the sufferings of
poets proscribed two continents away.
What could we write about? There's always love,

of course, and existential angst,
and picking up experimental threads
to be rewoven with a novel vengeance
into a resurrection of the dead.

And so we did. We made an avant-garde
out of our ancestors. We raised our banners
like bibles to intimidate the horde
with incantations of archaic honors.

And now a generation has arisen
that knew not Joseph, nor our years of thirst.
We wish them well. Let them be the chosen
for a change, and find a rhyme for *cursed*.

THE EXILE

Well before he died, the decree was repealed.
But after all, it made no difference to him.
"Home!" he would snarl, "Where should I call home?
The ground my parents lie buried in—that expelled

me? The land that landed me like a prize
flapping fish to show off their expertise
in political tolerance and the humanities?
Don't talk of home, please. It hurts my eyes."

His eyes hurt. He buried his head in his hands
and flew everywhere and sang in a dozen tongues
to keep from swallowing bile. Still, his lungs,
heart, guts—down to the Islets of Langerhans

detached and floated free in an endless ache.
Nothing connected to anything else. Horses
lashed to his limbs galloped in different directions. His torso
lay in its shivering skin on nostalgia's rack.

He married again. This time, a younger woman
of unimpeachable family and personal mystery
who worshiped him like Othello for his stories
and loved him for the thinning hair his demon

left scattered on pillows all around the world.
He hectored his students. Scorned his natural colleagues.
Kept in touch with his friends. Read only catalogues.
His opinions grew increasingly double-barrelled.

He died in a hotel room in a city he hated,
in a state whose name he'd never learned to pronounce.
Where he'd been born, they raised him monuments
As a great spokesman of the once-defeated.

⋮ NOW AND THEN ⋮

NOW AND THEN

Bodies surface in the bay
every now and then
bloated to anonymity.
We take them in.

We give them new names,
old wives
and comfortable homes
when they arrive

and try to make them talk.
They are steadfast
in their silence and their lack
of helpfulness.

Sooner or later we forget
their provenance.
Now and then an empty boat
bobs in the distance.

STATEMENT OF A REFUGEE FROM BABEL

What was most terrible was knowing
we were all saying the same thing.

The Last Great Poet of Sumer

for John Morressy

warns curly-bearded kings they are one flesh
        with Gilgamesh

who walked the walls and pronounced them sound
        but nowhere found

a builder's name burnt into the brick.
        Princes take

the poet's admonitions into their hearts,
        and he departs

laden with gold, meat, and an oily royal promise
        he will be famous

when the dry clay of their own titles has crumbled.
        The masters, humbled,

carve their deeds deep into generations of rock
        mounted block on block

by nameless slaves, while the nameless poet devours
        his portion within hours,

trades gold for passage on a barbarian ship
        and, safely boarded,
                falls asleep.

No Altarpiece

No altarpiece includes the painter
fronting the scene
from whom the weeping mother
turns, John shielding her
like a gangster's hat
from his quick eye.

He props his easel as the cross is set,
readies his first deft strokes,
half hearing cries
and registering their effect
unmoved among the crowd
before the light fails.

Later in the studio details
can be fleshed out,
colors deepened,
the perspective
of the thieves perfected,
qualities adjusted.

CNUT'S BOATSONG

When I row close by the shore
I can hear monks singing
Kyrie eleison
ely ely O

Wind and snow and winter storm
bring the year's hard beginning
Kyrie eleison
ely ely O

Come, fellow, bend an oar
home is where the bells ring
Kyrie eleison
ely ely O

The Dying Wolfram Laments His Life

I was a landsman in a guttural land
breathing umlauts in a courtly garden
before I crossed my armor with my pen
and came crusading with a warlike band
to match my wits against the Saracen.

Pricked by my own inspiring propaganda
of unresolvèd love and knightly glory,
I left the safety of my allegory
lying beside the languishing Amanda
to find the ghostly Sangraal of my story.

But now I've lost my stomach and my horse
to grim Sir Fever, liege of Paynim Plague,
and suffer from an unrelenting ague
offshore from Alexandria. Remorse
eats what the fever leaves—the rest is vague.

If God still loves me, with a Frankish pity
He kills me for His love and with one look
kindles to flame the falsehoods of my book,
and I shall live to see His Holy City
no more than Zazamanc or Azagouc.

An ardent landsman, I go cold at sea
in penance for those fictions that beguile
good Christian husbands into war and exile
far from unliberated Calvary.
I vomit content, going out of style.

THE APOLOGIE OF JOHN KETCH ESQ ; JULY 21, 1683

Sundry malicious rumours have been spread
      concerning my alleged misconduct when
I severed late Lord Russell from his head.
      I beg to put my case to decent men;
one story's good until another's told.

      Some say I drank the night before the blow,
and others, that I took Lord Russell's gold
      to make death quick, but aimed my short ax low,
then struck vindictively (and none too neatly)
      upon the shoulder, not behind the ear.

In truth, my Lord more nobly than discreetly
      had placed his arms where they might interfere
to fox my aim, and left his eyes untied.
      He felt the ax and flinched against the steel.
Such is the way William Lord Russell died.

      No man who knows my livelihood could feel
that I was either brutal or inept.
      I execute my business, nothing more.
My neighbours will bear witness that I slept
      as sober as a judge the night before.

SCHOLARSHIP

I bring good news:

The story of the peasant
who stole dust
from the emperor's grave
and was put to death
is a mistranslation
of the text.

DOCK SONG

(from the T'ang)

I took up with a broker
who tells a different story
at every market-bell.
I look at the tide
up and down the estuary
and wish I'd married a sailor.

AFTER EVER

for Tatiana Shcherbina

It was all inevitable, banal as a fairy-tale.
One day Snow White looked into her own eyes, saw
small lines that had stopped laughing, flesh drawn
in around a bony nose, and imagined
that the mirror itself recoiled,
looking for the sweet little stepdaughter
who had once glittered in its reflected light.

Doc was no help at all. Cosmetic surgery
would leave her wrapped in bandages for weeks
and not touch the nature of the disease: time.
All Prince could offer, his own sidelong glance
taking in the new second housemaid, was a holiday
somewhere quiet, where the sun wouldn't burn
its own brand of loveliness into her drying skin.

It was then she heard the huntsman again, smelled
ripe apples stewing among leaves in a cold cellar
and began studying old volumes for lore,
even comfort. She started a correspondence course
in oral history, learned at last about her sisters
with their failed strategies, the fisherman's cursed wife,
and sweet, ungifted, pin-pricked Sleeping Beauty.

But it was Medea's cauldron that tempted her.
All her life she had allowed herself to be cut up
into three hundred sixty-five pieces a year,
what did one or two more or less matter in the boil
if she could leap out again, bleating like a lamb?
She conjured up a chariot and dragons,
Killed what she could, and flew away to Athens.

WOMAN OF THE HIGH PLAINS

The ground boils here, but slowly—
not like the water in my pot
stripping a cooked chicken to bone
and soup, separable
identities. It takes,

they say, nine years or more
for a man to render down
to broth, and then his skeleton
can be picked out and thrown away.
My husband, now,

would pinch the soil each spring
and taste it for the planting,
knowing what it needed
until it needed him.

Riding the Reservoir

for Cola Franzen

Our governor's only help was, Pray for rain,
but prayers evaporated in the air.
The brightest comet in eight decades flared
overhead, and left a fading train

among our usual stars. My brother and I
rode the dry rim of the reservoir
watching abandoned landmarks reappear—
our old foundation muddy as a sty—

and half expecting, on the crazy mud
to find some private loss—a castaway
stuffed animal or forgotten wooden toy—
embedded at the bottom of the world.

For others' sake, we prayed each week for rain,
and, for our own, wished decades more of drought
to see what children's treasures brought to light
were fossilized for us in that terrain.

One day we walked a path we used to walk,
like astronauts the dark side of the moon,
attuned to every shadow in the stone
eroded by abundance and neglect,

and found, or thought we found, a little knoll
where we had sown a children's patch of corn,
the driveway of the house where we were born,
and that, for him, if not for me, was all.

Unlawful Entry

in memoriam Peter Boynton

No things but in things,
your self in shell and stone
displayed. This home
not yours, not ours, but some
way station where we met
and where you left your mark.

Eavesdroppers on the silence
of your absence, when we woke
the dark air was our game.

We start living in to it,
forget from where we took
this book down, where in clutter
that pencil lay with which
I write these lines.

We made mad love without once touching
and thought incessantly of you
whose house we tiptoed through
at gray, gray daybreak.

Relict

This one wrote for her man
verses as sickening as what wasted him
and shoveled him into his yankee mausoleum
of dust and root at twenty-nine.

She had them carved on slate
underneath the data of his life
commemorating herself a dutiful wife
who lost a proper mate.

She married again, we see
by stones less than a throw away,
and lived to know her second husband gray
or bald, and died at eighty-three

under a well-earned willow.
The dates are given by her name, no more,
no children, no hint of what she was married for
from the tight-lipped bedfellow

who outlived her a year
(whose marker mimics hers to the least detail
just when granite was coming into style)
perhaps himself too near

his own dead end to contemplate
his loss of her, perhaps unwilling to lie,
perhaps ineffably bereft, or merely
fashionably up-to-date

with an *In Memory of*
and not a single letter of mortality
suggesting to a buried curiosity
his buried love.

STONE RUBBING: A LOCAL GRAVEYARD

These black, faithful slaves who stand
through all weathers by their forgetful masters
at the open door, winged and grinning
and utterly submissive to my cold hand

will not leave off their warnings, prayers,
remembrances, even when I shroud them
and lift their souls into my own book.
Whatever I take, I leave what is most theirs.

I have been their gardener, their tender,
for my own end a servant to these servants
who care as little as their masters do
for anything less than apocalyptic splendor.

Who carved the slate felt for the dead

perhaps, and those who set the stone,
far more than my pathetic fallacies
can do, which take the cold death's head

and touch it every way but as my own.

THE AX-MURDERER'S DAUGHTER

The ax-murderer's daughter
got a brand-new yellow tutu
and satin slippers
for her eighth birthday.

And today is Every-Other-Saturday:
time to visit with her mother
where he lives ever since the accident
she was too young to remember
almost.

How she hates the long drive,
the iron doors and corridors,
the dirty little room where three bored men
watch her mother talking to him,
two girls fidgeting.

What is she supposed to think
about the stranger she's supposed to love
for her mother's sake and Jesus'?

She will stop visiting when she goes away to college
but write faithfully every month.

He will learn about her own two children, her divorce,
her move out of state, her new home.

She will give instructions to the chief of police
(there is always talk of budget-cutting,
of letting the safe ones out)
if ever he shows up in town:
Shoot on sight.

But today she will dance for him
in the dirty metal room to canned music
borrowed from her teacher.
She will wear her yellow tutu and satin slippers,
her mother, sister watching
and three bored guards.

And he will watch her, too, saying afterwards,
my little girl.
> *That's my little girl.*

MAN WITH A GUN

The man has no face.
The gun says
Give me all your money.
I have none.
Except for the jagged hole
the gun is speaking through
the window shows nothing
but my own reflection.
The gun has entered my house
like a man who sticks his head
through the cardboard cut-out
of a carnival photographer.
I am the tin lizzie
the grinning gun
is riding.

The gun says
Then give me that radio.
Will the gun let me go
and try and get it?
The radio is plugged
behind a heavy bookcase.
The gun is plugged
by an unspoken slug
into my back.
The radio won't fit
through the broken window.

The gun says
Make it snappy.
I snap a ruff of glass
around his neck
to make a space

wide enough to give him what he wants.
My fingers work precisely
because I am afraid
of mangling my hand.
I pass the radio
between the mullions.
The gun takes it
with one hand.

The gun says
I'm watching you
so don't move
for twenty minutes.
I wonder what's behind
my own reflection
disfigured by the hole
where my gut was.
I count twelve hundred sheep
without falling asleep.

FAULTY MEMORIES OF BIG JORDY

Over the years, in a movement inexorably glacial
hair had retreated before the passage of time
until the prehistoric wool of his head was all facial
and his skull, scoured, gleamed like a mountain-peak
over a timberline. His beard cascaded in rime
rimmed in untrimmed red over a caveman's chest.

If he were of a mind, he could heave a heavy sack
of goodies over his shoulder in the appropriate season
and play Saint Nick to all the neighborhood cub-pack—
but more often he kept to his own North Pole, dressed
in a torn t-shirt and always with the same dungarees on
as if these were a medicine bag holding all his luck.

From an upstairs window I watched him once, digging a hole
in the sandy ground, for a purpose I never determined.
He dug and dug all day long, and the sand displaced in a pile
surrounded him like a boy's fort in a backyard war.
He found no gold, perhaps a piece or two of broken china,
but he took nothing away of what he was digging for.

He ran every road-race the island offered, lumbering along
like a steam locomotive indifferent to the lanky contenders
who drank mixed drinks after their exertions, eyeing the bartender.
He walked the beaches all night sometimes, singing his own soft song,
for there was a gentleness in him he never let on to in town
where his ex-wife lay dying slowly in the arms of another man.

He climbed trees and peered through the windows of startled girls
undressing for bed. Caught, he pleaded that old excuse, love.
He never begged a single penny that I know of,
and slept, if he slept at all, the way a stunsail or a housecat furls.
Nobody cared for him—but like history or genetics, he was ours.
One night he dropped something, and wafted off to the stars.

Urban Revitalization

Girls snap bubblegum in the brick mall
In the old millworks.
They wander through a transparent front,
Finger twill and study the fall
Of a season's fashion, wander out again
To bum cigarettes by the fast food.

Clouds of cotton dust hang like tobacco
In the murky air of blackened red brick.
Girls catch the death of it between their teeth
On parched tongues, dreaming a dollar a day,
The kindly glance of a handsome supervisor,
Smashing the boss's face in.

Girls flick butts into a new fountain
Of recycled water, a closed circuit,
Conditioned air and canned music,
Eye the boys bussing cheap tables
Where girls mind the clack of machinery,
Sort out long, doubled threads,
And count sixteen standing hours until dinner
In a dim boarding house down the street

Where their mothers wait, wondering,
And their silent grandmothers, remembering.

Lacrimæ Rerum / Before First Period

She came down, thundering on the stair,
crying with all her heart, "What shall I wear?"
and the whole house echoed her despair.

The heavens gave no help, ambiguous
temperature, gray cumulo-strato-cirrus,
silent—whatever—with nothing to say to us.

Still she dressed, ate breakfast, and said goodbye,
shouldered her pack. Outside, looked up. The sky
dropped a single tear into her eye.

1972–1989

She went to death like a pampered cat
unable to abide a closed door.
Out of fabled curiosity she scratched
and cried until it opened for her
and she hurtled down the dark stair.

THE TRANSLATOR

—Lawdy, Miz Scarlett! I don know nuffin bout birfin babies!
—Tear him for his bad verses!

This is to say, I have misunderstood.
This is to say, I ha   ve made mistakes.
I am, so to speak, Cinna the poet—
the wrong sinner, the textual error
for whom the rock won't cleave, the sea
won't translate red into green
(it is only my own blood, after all).

This is to say, I am still wrestling
with one word in your first stanza
that means nothing but itself, like you.
This will go on till morning—
and from it my achievement
is a new name and a permanent limp;
yours, a reputation for mystery.

This is to say, there is nothing here
to match that movie-line of yours;
thus, I am tempted (I confess) to footnote:
The comic servant confesses fraud
at a time of ultimate crisis, when nothing else
but expert skill will do to bring a brat
into a burning world. This is to say

nothing of substance. I am Cinna, sinnerman.
Rend Caesar into what is Caesar's,
untangle the fancy words and find
somewhere between the lines a cryptic
map of the catacombs of Babel,
the treasure of definitive translation:
All will be forgiven, understood.

⋄ DESIRES ⋄

DESIRES

We talked all night long about writing—
the fat woman, you and I and the blonde
student I wouldn't mind getting alone
for a weekend: Gretchen to my Faust.

We talked all night long about writing
and it snowed like hell but didn't stick.
The blonde girl said she wanted medical
coverage, and the fat woman wanted kids.

We talked all night long about writing,
and I know what you want is recognition
with faculty status and a book
or two like stiff drinks under your belt,

and I'd take the same, either way,
but what I wouldn't mind more than anything
are words set down to make a difference
to me, to the fat woman and the blonde girl

and, of course, to you, but not just you.
We talked all night long about writing
like characters in somebody's famous book
dedicated to the author's wife.

CHIEF JOY

"If I do not remember thee, let my tongue cleave to the roof of my mouth; if I prefer not Jerusalem above my chief joy."

Christ! I wish I could write in Irish,
deal down rhymes to rout black rats,
harp on the wind across green fields
and glory in heroes with singing shields—
I curse my father for the name of Katz.

Jesus, I'd like to write in English
and carol the queen of the azure snood,
or chase rare birds and country maids
and sigh to death when the twilight fades—
but I've been cheated, screwed, and jewed.

Father omnipotent! Welsh and Scottish
straitlaced lines my tongue could savor
and sing in kirk or chapel I'd
prefer in my mouth on a stony hillside
instead of this licorice eastern flavor.

I hear America singing, Lord,
the lawless songs of a thousand tribes,
hymning and humming in rhythms of jazz
the wonders of new Utopias
and scorn for pharisees and scribes.

Israel, hear my present anguish—
forgive me for the craft of longing.
The promise is no substitute
for certain country underfoot
and the impossible belonging.

THE STRINGS

O how she openly embraces music I would be the instrument between
her legs her fingers on my mellow strings my scroll along her shoulder
and a single point against her arch to hold me steady while she plays I
swell and taper

Barrel pirate of my adolescence now I hear him clumping on behind
me muttering in a honeyed baritone good counsel graveled warnings
life is hard and slow and resonant for one alone and dangerous in
company weigh every measure

Prodigious on the shrill heights he dives a schoolboy at the quarry
in July over and over in the cold and oily water at the rockfoot never
dipping far below the bright surface where ice rises over abandoned
machinery

Always a step in the background she is one whose face in the
photograph is hidden she has turned to hear her neighbor's whisper
stooped to soothe a fretful child I have looked for her recall her easy
frequent smile

THE CONSOLATIONS OF LITERATURE

Down a cold telephone line what can I say?
How am I doing? Doing *well enough,*
doing a little here and there, some stuff—
What else is there since: *you are away.*
What can I add to that? Yeah, I'm *okay*
(a little less than truth and more than bluff)
but if you want professions off the cuff
of hungry passion, read Louise Labé
(as I am doing late at night) *Oh, where
are you, my love, my very soul? Do not
abandon me, your body, to the restless bed
stripped of the breath itself we used to share.
Lifeless I lie until my soul is brought
back to a breathing corpse you left for dead.*

BOSTON MUSEUM OF FINE ARTS

Today is Sunday. The museum is free.
I leave you sleeping in your lotus-blue
synthetic empire-waisted *robe de nuit*
and go to gaze on loveliness not you:
the plunder of the gods, the arrogance
of kingdoms and collectors set in view
to serve a bland eclectic reverence
when I have nothing secular to do.
Here, like a birder in his favorite swamp,
I keep an eye out for what I can find
among the color, delicacy and pomp.
I have no special masterpiece in mind,
but let myself be caught by wing and wing,
indifferent to the lore of humankind.
No single room collects me. Everything
competes to keep my vision unconfined.
Ibis, Brancusi, Persian hawk-and-duck,
Gauguin's strange, stupid bird are commonplace
in the unchecked profusion of my luck—
until I've had enough of captive grace
and long to try my skill at venery
with certain pleasure in the steady chase.
Seeking a prize, I close my eyes and see
your lotus body, your Egyptian face
in that one room where I most want to be.

THE CHERUBIM

*"When Israel used to make the pilgrimage, they would roll up for
them the Parokhet, and show them the Cherubim which were inter-
twined with one another, and say to them: 'Behold! your love before
God is like the love of male and female!'"*

—RAB QETINA

That room at the museum, the one
with the Etruscan tombs—you know
I've taken other women there
(before I met you, years ago)
and stood in the conditioned air
to watch the couples carved in stone

embracing naked on a bed
of pitted rock as easily
as if they had no fear at all
in their forgotten history
of leaving everything we call
worthwhile and good, of being dead.

Where living animals grow fat,
we've looked at shapeless megaliths
scattered around the pastureland.
The clumsy stones of country myths
show us a death we understand.
We could accept an end like that

if not for the Etruscans where
they rest together side by side—
one couple not yet done with life,
the other a bridegroom and bride—
conveying all that man and wife
in artificial space can share.

In just this way have you and I
lain after love in foreign rooms,
in open fields, one cloistered park,
on beaches, in our private homes,
in privacies of light and dark
like practicing sarcophagi

or like (they say) the Cherubim
both male and female who enclosed
the dwellinghouse of God, entwining
limbs and torsoes in a pose
as intimate as yours and mine.

I wonder what became of them.

Life Story

for Jeff Schwartz

I know the story, how
the spider mates and dies
and then the old haymow
is thick with spiders,

how in generic terms
there is no death, and life
cleaves to starfish and worms
under the knife,

how the word just learned
appears in every paragraph
until it is burned
like a lover's epitaph

into the brain, how
even a stupid passion will
not be killed, but now
in a blizzard of fine silk

will fasten its filaments
and dormant seed
on any object for the chance
to breed.

To an Irish Landlady

Mrs. M—, your sniffing disapproval
       of lust under your lease is well and good.
No straight-limbed gentleman at large will cavil
       at allowing as you're doing what one should,
or doubt that rectitude keeps out the Devil
       (who's snarling somewhere in the neighborhood
and looking sharp for landladies to pounce on,
while lovers like us can always find beds to bounce on).

But O, thou flaming angel of the sword!
       Something is rotten on the brink of Eden
when pleasure, not just decently deplored,
       is publicly deprived a bed to breed in.
Can carnal bliss be righteously abhorred
       by any but that Lord who put the seed in
in the first place? This is high divinity,
and not just argument about rent and virginity.

So, while we two with wandering step and slow
       from Dublin take our intertwining way,
we chant this curse along the road we go:
       May you, when night is longer than the day,
hear giggles in your sleep and "oh, oh, OH"
       from that cold room where we had loved to lay;
may you lie henceforth sleepless till the dawn
rouse you from waking dreams you hate to dwell upon;

and may your fingers (when you next seek sleep)
        inch under bedclothes in between your thighs,
caress, explore, and in recesses creep
        with restless purpose and a vague surmise;
may you hold dear what you consider cheap
        and cheapen yet with territorial cries,
and ride all night, unsatisfied, the hand
that now you raise against us in your lovely land.

ROBBING THE BANK

The fat pig sits where it always sat,
splotched with terracotta florets,
one ear broken off, three-legged.

In the old days my young wife,
squealing, held the pig upside down
while I worked a table knife
gently into the slot, back and forth,
until all the pennies cascaded
and we went out to eat.
The pig never grew lean.

Time for the knife.

Wheaters slide down the blade
like blood, dimes and nickels
trickle along, the occasional quarter:
indigestible Lyndon sandwiches.

Money comes slowly
when you have to hold the pig yourself
and handle the knife yourself.

A few Susan B. Anthonies clink,
a hope-chest of Kennedy half-dollars,
and ringing silver from before the economy turned over,
from before the marriage went sour,
when the pig was still young.

THE NEW BRIDGE

They built it of unmortared stone
and started calling it the New Bridge.
Later, the older, wooden ones
burned to the water's edge—

one by one, in their own time
and not without replacement.
But the New Bridge kept its name
downstream from concrete abutment

and suspended steel. And still
in my heart I call you lover
though even the river has silted full
and changed its course forever.

AWAY

Last night I walked away from a woman.
She stood backlit in the doorway
and I looked away from her, at the moon
full and low in the sky.

After goodnight, there was nothing to say.
Tomorrow she will see her son
who has been away a month in the mountains
almost entirely on his own.

I drove home. It was a long drive,
longer than by daylight. The moon
blinded me whenever the road curved
and I had to meet it head on.

Envoy

Between women I forget the phases of the moon.
I no longer dance that monthly attendance.
Sometimes I am surprised how much it has changed
since I last looked: It is newer, or it is older.
And when it isn't there at all I miss
all those who have touched me with their white light.

Dawn Song

O body, we lie here locked
in an inseparable embrace
while hands circle the clock face
twelve times faster than the sun
like a lover's deliberate chase
over another's body.

It is second best to lie alone
in bed, but to be rung out
like an old year every morning at
the same time is worst of all—
thinking of the chopped dreams
we drop in a second

when the alarm sounds. Body,
I am already up, gone
into the world you brood on,
spitefully dragging you with me
to shower in the cold dawn
naked, shivering, arm in arm.

I Used To Sing

I used to sing when winter set me free
from summer and a falling off. No more.
The drifts that crowded you are smothering me.

Sometimes I'd hike the river, sometimes ski
where snow lay drifted thick along the shore.

I used to sing when winter set me free
from school, and I could take the time to be
a Scott or Peary, eager to explore
the drifts that crowded.
                                   You are smothering me,
snow-blind, in ways I never could foresee.

Can you remember how it was before?
I used to sing when winter set me free—
we'd sit inside together, knee to knee,
and harmonize the apple-fire's roar.

The drifts that crowded you are smothering me.
The fire spits cold for lack of apple-tree
and snow is banking up against the door.

I used to sing when winter set me free.
The drifts that crowded you are smothering me.

WHEN YOU RETURNED

When you returned rich and swaggering
from the discovery of yourself,
unwilling to surrender sovereignty,
I felt an empire tremble.

WEAPONS

How many objects
around the house
will do for weapons?
Have we tried them all?

We have flung books
and food, of course,
and whatever happens
to tumble when we pull—

ideas and facts,
compassion and remorse,
receipts and coupons,
sex and will—

of all our effects
none is harmless.
This axe I sharpen
is an eight-pound maul.

OUT

Everything will, you know. The bone
harp singing in the king's hall,
the cunning wound, tobacco-stained
carpeting, a telephone call,

Col. Mustard in the dining room
with a wrench, Raskolnikov
in existential gloom,
brothers wrestling over a pocketknife

on a slippery riverbank,
strangers stretched on their knees.
Fingering a pistol, jilted Frankie
nails Johnnie in his BVDs.

That's how it is: What we act
in private becomes the matter
of music, the marrow of related fact
in a storyteller's patter,

and nothing we can dream is left
without beforehand or afterwards
unaccounted for. When we laughed,
our laughter was broadcast by the birds,

and when you slammed the door
an old shaman in a weatherbeaten tent
half the world away finished the story
and told me where you went.

AIR

Atoms disperse, they say, around the world.
Each one of us inspires with every breath
Socrates' sigh, Napoleon's wild oath,
and a high C that Pavarotti held

when he brought down the house in Buenos Aires.
For sure, the selfsame oxygen that burned
in Sappho's breast has turned and been returned
from ooze to ozone in the wildest airs.

In front of me, set on a wooden stand,
a souvenir, an iridiscent sphere
made while we crowded at a country fair
around the artist, easy to my hand,

holds in its fragile glass the breath of all
of the above, and seven billion others
with unknown names, who aspirated ethers
ready mixed—and which contains as well

the life of him who crafted it to be
the little world it is. Most precious brew
of cosmic gases, and among them you
commingled with the universe and me.

HARVEST OF THE FIELDS

Translations

Gaius Valerius Catullus

34

Dianæ sumus in fide . . .

True to Diana's honor
We, her virgin boys and girls,
To Diana sing, we virgin
      Boys and girls.
O mighty daughter of Latona
And of almighty Jupiter,
Born underneath the olive
      On Delos,
Mistress of the mountain,
Of greenwood and of glen,
And of the echoing stream
      Running through,
Diana at the Crossroads,
Juno in the birthing-room,
Everchanging Luna
      All are you—
Measuring the months
The whole year round,
Gathering the harvest
      Of the fields,
As you have always blessed
The progeny of Romulus
With your holy name
      Stand by us.

Quintus Horatius Flaccus

ODE 1:4

Solvitur acris hiems grata vice veris et favoni . . .

(To Sestius)

Bitter winter this year is finally cracked open
by the south wind. Fishing boats slide down their rails
into the lake. Livestock kick at the barn-door
to get into pastures turning green.

There will be dancing now lit by the moon,
you'll feel the softened ground shake under the feet
of magical girls circling hand in hand
heedless of distant thunder.

Now is the time to go after flowers, and pick
your sacrifices for the burgeoning year.
Whatever the gods ask for, a lamb or a kid
dedicated to the shadowy groves.

Colorless death kicks in the door of a hovel
as quick as a royal bastion. O my fortunate friend,
the span of life is too small to keep adding hope on hope.
Night crowds in, with its storied ghosts,

and that echoless realm of the dead, where wine
has no taste and the dice are all blank, and where
you are indifferent to Lycidas, stud that he is,
keeping the young girls warm.

Richard Plantagenet, Cœur de Lion

LAMENTATION IN CAPTIVITY

Ja nus on pris ne dira sa raison . . .

No captive ever will speak true and well
Unless in sadness, but he can dispel
His grief in song, for comfort in his cell.
I have a thousand friends, who all excel
In shameful thrift, leaving me here to dwell
Two years a prisoner.

My barons and my men learned long ago,
Lords of England, Normandy, Bordeaux,
That I would not leave one of them in woe
For want of money, locked in this château.
I speak without reproach or wrath, although
I am a prisoner.

This have I learned from loneliness herein:
The dead and captive have no friend nor kin,
Since I am left by earl and paladin
For gold and silver. Great is my chagrin
For those who, when I die, will bear the sin
Of leaving me a prisoner.

It is no miracle my heart is sore.
My own protector wracks my land with war.
If he recalled his obligation, or
Honored the solemn compact that we swore,
It would not be so very long before
I were no more a prisoner.

They know, each lord of Gaul and Albion
Who, rich in health and gold, beholds the sun,
How much I grieve in foreign garrison.
They loved me well, their love is all fordone.
Our plains will never ring with glories won
      While I am a prisoner.

Go, little song, and tell them once again,
Those whom I loved and love—The Saracen
Could not be more unfaithful than these men.
With all my heart, how I would storm this den
If they—Bastards! Turning against me when
      I remain a prisoner.

Anonymous

Two Songs

1

Bele Yolanz en chambre coie . . .

Lovely Yolande sits in her room at ease,
A silken cloak spread out across her knees,
Plying the golden thread as if to please
Her mother, who does not like what she sees:
                "I'm warning you, Yolande!

Simpering miss, I have a thing to say
To you and, if I can, girl, then I may."
"What do you have in mind, Mamà, today?"
"I'll tell you in my own deliberate way—
                I'm warning you, Yolande!"

"Mamà, get on with it. what are you stewing
About? Is it my manners or my sewing?
Don't I keep my mouth closed while I'm chewing?
Am I too lazy? What have I been doing?"
                "I'm warning you, Yolande!

It's not your sleeping or embroidery
Or eating habits that are bothering me,
But that I think you talk too favorably
And much too often with the Count Mahì.
                I'm warning you, Yolande!

You laugh with him, you let him touch your hand
As if by accident, but it's all planned.
It's weighing very heavily on your husband.
You better stop it now, my dear Yolande.
                    I'm warning you, Yolande!"

"Oh, let my husband swear and stamp and shout
For all his relatives who hang about—
The law is on his side, I have no doubt,
But, after all, my feelings will come out."
                    "Just watch yourself, Yolande!"

        2

Quand vient en mai, que l'on dit as lons jors ...

In May-time when the light is lingering,
The lords return from following their king,
And Raynault foremost in their company.
But when they pass where Erembour can see,
He turns his head, and will not say a thing.
                    "Oh, Raynault, my love!"

Erembour at her window's narrow light
Sits with her sewing, watching every knight.
She sees them all come riding from the king,
And foremost, Raynault downcast, saying nothing.
She cries to him from her protected height,
                    "Oh, Raynault, my love,

My dear Raynault, the way it was before,
When you rode proudly past my father's door,
You would have suffered if I had not spoken."
"Princess, to my shame! Now you have broken
The trust between us. There is nothing more—"
                    "Oh, Raynault, my love!

What lies these are your lordship apprehends!
I call upon the witness of my friends
And swear by all the saints that I have never
Loved anyone but you, nor will I ever.
I have a kiss for you, to make amends,
                    Oh, Raynault, my love!"

The Count Raynault has climbed the castle stair.
His form is slim, his shoulders broad, his hair
Curly blond—let Erembour understand
There's no such other man in all the land.
She sighs to look at him, so strong and fair,
                    "Oh, Raynault, my love!"

The Count Raynault is in her room and seated
At last beside her on her flowery bed,
And there the Count Raynault and Erembour
Renew the love they had begun before . . .
*   *   *   *   *   *

                    "Oh, Raynault, my love!"

Olivier de Magny

SONNET

"Hola, Charon, Charon, Nautonnier Infernal!"

Hey there, Charon, Charon, you ferryman to Hell!
Who is it who summons me with such insistent fervor?
It is the exhausted, weeping spirit of a faithful lover,
Who has suffered only ill for loving all too well.
What do you want of me? Passage across your river.
What is the cause of death? A question all too cruel!
It is Love that killed me. *Into the dark valley*
I will never ferry those whom Love commands, not ever.
Charon, for pity's sake, please receive me in your boat.
Look for another pilot, because neither I nor Fate
Defies this master of the Gods, he whom all must fear.
I will go in spite of you, for within my soul
Love has such dominion and my eyes so many tears
That I will be the river, and the ferry, and the pole.

Gérard de Nerval

DELFICA

La connais-tu, Dafné, cette ancienne romance, . . .

Daphne, are you familiar with this antique singing,
Under the sycamore, or white laurel buds,
Under the olive, myrtle, or trembling willow heads,
This balladry of love . . . always a new beginning!

Do you recognize the *temple* with its immense arcade,
And the sour lemons that have set your teeth on edge?
And the grotto, fatal to the feet of careless pilgrimage,
Where the conquered dragon oversees its sleeping seed.

Those Gods you keep on mourning will once again arise!
Time will bring back the rituals of those former days;
The earth already shivers with a breath of prophecies . . .

And the sibyl with her old Italian eyes, all this while
Under the Arch of Constantine in enchanted sleep still lies:
And nothing yet disturbs the unembellished peristyle.

Jacques Prévert

BLOOD ORANGE

La fermeture éclair a glissé sur tes reins . . .

The zipper slid down your flank
and the whole providential storm of your body in love
in the midst of shadows
suddenly exploded
And your dress slipping to the waxed tiles
made no more noise
than an orange-peel falling on a rug
But under our feet
its tiny mother-of-pearl buttons crackled like seeds
Blood orange
fruit of delight
The point of your breast
drew a new luck-line
in the palm of my hand
Blood orange
Fruit of delight

Sun in the night.

René Daumal

Madam Midnight

Madame Minuit meurt de désespoir . . .

Madam Midnight dies of despair
each time she hears like a hammer of wind
the sudden breath of the Little Black King
sounding on the marble stair.

Her gold-fed fingers stroke the fur
on the nape of the pussycat in her lap
who warms her paws and turns her back
to the icy wind in the corridor.

The Little Black King, perched in gloom,
slowly turns the black pig loose,
and the glutinous sop of What's-the-Use
quiets the dogs in the anteroom.

He has made the cat his confederate
with a gift of gold. She turns her eyes
to the gallery, and Madam dies
under the dark paw of her pet.

Evgeny Saburov

WHO IS NOT OZYMANDIAS?

Ну, кто из нас не Озимандия? Ну, кто не Царь царей?

Who is not Ozymandias? Which of us is not the King of kings?
Ever since Gutenberg gave Europe a Far Eastern
plaything, we are no longer timebound,
but time itself is afraid of us,
we have become more long-lived than the seas.

So, what's to say here! On ribbons of film-stock
all history is winged, like victory,
and our brutalized descendants teach
about grandpa's and his pàpa's power and glory.

What's this Ozymandias? Be quiet, then,
a textbook approved for secondary schools
for the unexplored regions of the soul,
a magician just as good as sand.

Alexey Shelvakh

REQUIEM

Умер однажды советский поэт . . .

A real Soviet poet gave up the ghost
And left an opening in the host.

Alas, old age caused him to die—
Far better had it been you or I.

Three in one the wide world loses:
Insider, chairman, minion of muses.

A composer according to Party lines—
Who now will enlighten people's minds?

In a thundering herd or a docile flock,
You sang us all to the chopping block.

Miners laboring in their veins
Received the blessing of your strains.

The harvesters your words repeat
As they gather in the wheat.

You tried your best to blunt the tooth
And dim the eye of hopeful youth.

You kept to your given time and place
And played for the future's saving grace.

How hard you worked, your pen your spade!
What a hole in literature you made!

Sergey Magid

Paradise County Seat[1]

> *Thrown together for so many centuries*
> *with foreigners, the inhabitants of Pæstum*
> *have forgotten the Greek tongue. . . .*
> *They repeated Greek words out loud*
> *which now only a few barely understood. . .*
> *For they remembered that they too were Greeks. . .*
> *And now? See where have they fallen long ago*
> *and among whom, so alien and far away.*
>
> — K. CAVAFY, "THE INHABITANTS OF PAESTUM"[2]

> *. . . love of a country*
> *Begins as attachment to our own field of action.*
> — T. S. ELIOT, "FOUR QUARTETS"

в этом доме мы жили прежде чем умереть . . .

1

the house we lived in, waiting to die, this is it
you carried me up and down these stairs in your arms
neither of us understanding how people pick at each other
while time is a battering ram

       or a quiet landslide in the mountains.

2

this is the house where you carried me when I broke my leg
where we were never alone among a myriad of strangers
like glass doors we looked through into each other's eyes

---

1 *The Russian title is a bureaucratic word meaning "regional administrative center,"
but it also contains a pun on the Russian word for "paradise." The pun is common
and, of course, ironic.*
2 *Rae Dalven's translation, slightly altered to conform more closely with Magid's
Russian version.*

before you moved away
beyond all the watch-faces
that stare into my own face

maybe you've found your own place at last
on the pendulum's backbone
now that you're what
time's pivot
is made of
or maybe you've expanded through the universe
the eternal figure-eight of an hourglass
tipped on its side
filling up all the traversible space out there

    3

I couldn't step across Bolshoy Prospekt[1]
I couldn't get across it at all
it was rush-hour in the evening, non-stop
too many people, too many women, too many cars
the crowd elbowed me aside
illuminated windows
a cold rain
I hadn't a clue what to do with myself
once again it all came to an end
and started up at last again
life

in a space equidistant from every tollgate
and from the silence in every voice
in an autumnal void at the tip of Vasily Island[1]

---

1 *Bolshoy Prospekt, Vasily Island : a major thoroughfare and a neighborhood in Leningrad.*

4

here in this house from time to time
everyone enjoyed the good health
of a pistol in its holster
and from time to time here in this house
everyone was right except me—not me
and a voice off the radio slithered languidly like a boa constrictor
and time polished its spectacles like a serpent
to look us over in the details of our fear

when—a woodchuck at the mouth of its burrow—
you stood in the doorway
while the chuckling city pulled a trigger
and the anchorman's voice droned on like a centenarian tortoise

my rhymes are elevator-simple
my rhythm primitive, language approximate
the drift of my thinking has long been suspect
like Jonathan Swift

but my memory is precise: you said *my son*
and no one now alive can say that to me—
not Yurin summoned by three rings; not Davidoff, by two; not Rebko, by one.[1]

5

for the lost, there is always the planet
a lonely paradise, a center of local government
with all the values of the Technological Revolution
with a million-year-old complaint
welling up in our words

_____

1 *Doorbell signals for summoning different residents of a communal apartment.*

6

upstairs and down we ran races

7

when you were forty and I was ten
now, I am forty and you—the remainder
forever invisible to us

8

but something is glittering out there, out there
in the hollow, dialectical fog
something rustling like a cotton towel
the heart of a fellow-traveler or the whisper of a second-class citizen
or the voice of a child deep in 1931

"Daddy, look!
why is that guy lying in the road,
that guy at the side of the road
and nobody's helping him up?"

"Why can't I be a hawk, why don't I fly?"[1]

And in 1919, a bored horseman
from the wild division[2] burst into the house
("Tell me, Daddy, why can't I be a hawk?")
where grandpa in his tallis is praying to their god
and from the back wall to the doorsill life stopped

---

1 *A line from a Ukrainian folk song.*
2 *A division of the Russian army in World War I and after, composed primarily of*
Caucasian volunteers

and god dwells only in the body—beyond that, nothing but caesar,
the ubiquitous chameleon-individual
This patriotic horseman, protector of russia
here he stands in the doorway, glowers
spits out like a spew of tobacco-juice
only a single word, but what a word!
and how many guys are buried in its sound:
"Jew?"

9

god gets god's due. But what to caesar?
life?
what of the right to breathe?
every gasp is a dime; a half-gasp, a penny
you pay out every day
faith?
this is our mother
who bore you, and in whose name you will die.
a little gold?
you'll find it tucked with luck
inside the soul.
and—the soul?
to what end that tatter of breath?
the soul is the lead in a pencil
we use to scribble out our existence.
caesar keeps quiet and waits.
he is forbearing, our caesar,
in the sense that he bears our smell and sweat.
Grandpa's dry response: "I'm a glazer."

They say the horseman was caught by surprise
he wiped the old blood off his blade
scowled and unexpectedly choked out
from his throat, like a cat: "Then live!"

10

it was up these stairs you bore me from the maternity ward

11

no, not you. I remember different hands.
Whose? Who stands there behind the door?
My brother practicing zen à la suzuki?
An old friend researching the church fathers?
An alky-head classmate with an electric drill?
If I could choose—who? Anyone at all?
Them all?
A casual passerby?
But not you. Why?
Why does everything turn out like this?

12

one as good as the next, each one
able to fill the same space
one after another they come
in their thirst

think of it. In the whole metagalaxy
this is the only place without special privileges
And we're not ready for winter
And, as usual,
the water's been shut off

13

Grandpa glazed windows for the entire neighborhood.
He polished everything. Before sleep he chatted with the cats
and his difficult god, just as tenderly
forgiving those and That One. He raised cherry trees
and seven children.
Dear Comrade:
In reply to yours of the ult.
the City Council regrets to inform you
that the evidence of a certain witness
Comrade Davidova
confirms the killing of your parents
father and mother by fascist barvarians
like thousands of other Soviet people.

who is to say this is not poetry?
vers libre penned in 1943
who was it saw my grandfather?
you? the woman over here?
that man who lived through hell?

14

by the way, there are two versions:
in one,
they were hanged
head downward from a kharkov balcony
in the other
buried alive
where even now,
quicksand ripples *stormclouds*
race, stormclouds spin;

an invisible moon illuminates
the flying snow;
a murky sky,
the night is murky.
I ride, I ride through the empty field,
the harness-bells go din-din-din
fearful
fearfully out of control
across an unknown plain[1] I am singing a hymn

15

to love.
In Achaia the day is overcast.
The world in its cage of meridians pecks at grain.
These are the hollow streets. This is Pnom Penh.
The drunken poet in the Rotonde slowly savors his Pernod.
Meanwhile it grows peppery light
and the dawn sky is a Salvador Dali landscape.
Beyond the television screen—but this is 2041
and far
far away, nearly to dusty Mars—
If you look into the deeps from the here of night and light
and an island like a yellow leaf in the mouth of a brook,
you will see how the cooling wake
the planet carves through the cold belongs to no one at all.
The paradise county seat of oxygen is up in the cheap seats,
a gallery over the abyss, a galley in the deep laughter of darkness,
a Khazar Sharukan and, over it, a Ukrainian balcony

_____

1 *Lines from Pushkin's "Demons."*

on which I begin—and "I" means "we."
Yes, we are all Scythians,[1] as the man said when he sang his farewell,
meaning something completely different, of course, completely different,
but making the point.
If the Universe is an amphitheatre
then each of us bleaches in our own row
in Achaia.

the day continues overcast.
On the sleepy coat-hangers of rivers hang city claim-checks.
In the fall, the windows are bloodless, and Pnom Penh, ward boss,
settles Brooklyn cinder by cinder in the new quarters of Leningrad.
So who's looking at us—who sends us messages
shooting pictures by oblique moonlight
having learned us by heart, just as we are
on this rainy night.
I am singing a hymn to love. Grain grows on the stars.
The city is light as a cherry—No? Then ponder it.
Once again life has slipped through the zero-point.
Give us this day our daily bread.
I am singing a hymn to love. Da-da, da-da.
I am singing a hymn to love. Da-da, da-da.
I am singing a hymn to love. Da.

> *September 1987*
> *Leningrad*

---

1 *A line from Alexandr Blok's "Scythians."*

Aleksandra Sozonova

His Wife Is a Suicide

А у него жена — самоубийца

His wife is a suicide.
He sits on the bed and rolls a cigarette.
He says, "I thought I understood."
He crumples a handful of blanket.

Then he stands up and opens the door.
He steps out into the snow.
Stripping down, he makes a deal:
White for naked, naked for white.

He wades in, arrays himself in snow,
Falls into snow, lies down, face to the sky,
The warmth of a single dream
In the hushing of his brain:

"Get rid of the memory. All of it. Hurry . . ."

Clench the pen in a calloused hand.
What a wide space opens up, what freedom.
Room for unsatisfied thought,
Sensitive to the cold.

A field has opened, night and snow have opened up.
The open sky . . . is a black page.
Breathing is difficult in the gloom
And all this open space.

Nikolai Baitov

LANDSCAPE WITH IDEAS FROM DOSTOEVSKY

Обычная картина. Мост . . .

An ordinary picture. Over a steep bank
a steel bridge soared like an arrow.
A business-like diesel locomotive
pulled its weight of boxcars and tankers,

when suddenly, right in the middle, it
collided with a high-strung suburban local.
The cars up-ended—hence the usual
terror of travelers caught in disaster.

And the crippled freight, not free from
the tragical game being played out,
broke through the railings of the bridge
and plunged into the innocent little stream,

where a motorboat, just at this very moment,
not suspecting any kind of dirty trick,
yawning lightly under strains of music
and carrying a load of Sunday drunks . . .

while right overhead, something jammed
the propeller of a helicopter, which fearfully
attempts to fall into the same pile-up
among the burning, drowned and maimed.

An ordinary, everyday subject for art . . .
But suddenly from the bushes, parting twigs,
a certain western-minded, petty journalist
has flashed the spiteful lens of a camera!

Arsen Mirzaev

O LUDMILA!

Нынче верх берут уроды . . .

These days the freaks are taking over.
These days nothing works, Ludmila.
Nature's given up on weather.
Even water runs uphill.

A little drizzle. Crying cat.
This morning I rolled out of bed
(an empty feeling in my gut)
and fell on the unlucky side.

Women sang to catch my ear.
Musicians filed into church.
Pigeons settled in my hair—
couldn't find a better perch.

After that, a rising moon
glittered from a long way off.
And someone's eyes. And you were gone,
Ludmila, but I played it tough.

Not crying yet, I keep my cool.
That's how I am, right on top.
Between the two of us, I'm still
smart and strong and acting up.

Notes on the Translations

Gaius Valerius Catullus (1st c. B.C.E.), born in Verona, flourished in Rome, and is best known for his various poems of satire and passion, of which this is not one.

Quintus Horatius Flaccus (65–8 B.C.E.), born in Venusia, studied in Rome and Athens, wrote verse letters, satires and lyric poems. The ode translated here is one of his most popular and frequently translated.

Richard Plantagenet (1157–1199) wrote this "Lamentation" while he was a prisoner in Dürenstein, the hostage of Leopold V of Austria. His liege lord (by Richard's title as Count of Anjou) was his fellow Crusading king, Philip II of France.

Anonymous ("Two Songs"). A number of anonymous (or not — five are ascribed to one Audefroi the Bastard) "songs of weaving" from the late 12th and early 13th century survive. Whether or not they were actually composed by the women who sang them at the loom is a matter of conjecture. Although the last full line of "Raynault" is often presented as missing, I'm convinced that the music alone fully carries the message.

Olivier de Magny, born in Cahors in 1529 or 1530, served as secretary to King Francis I and took part in a diplomatic mission to Rome along the way of which he met (and reportedly became a lover of) Louise Labé in Lyons. He returned to his post in France and died in 1561.

Gérard de Nerval (1808–1855) was an early French Romantic poet and novelist, and the translator of Goethe's *Faust*. "Delfica" is one in a sequence of a dozen mystic sonnets, *Les Chimères*.

Jacques Prévert (1900–1977) was a popular French poet and screenwriter. I translated "Blood Orange" originally, decades ago, as a class exercise for Norman R. Shapiro, who himself has translated a large "sampler" of Prévert's poetry, *Préversities* (Black Widow Press, 2010).

René Daumal (1908–1944) was a minor avant-garde French poet far better known as an experimental novelist with mystic proclivities.

Evgeny Saburov (1946–2009), born in Yalta, was a poet and playwright. He pursued a distinguished career as an economist and a bank director, including a stint as minister of economics in Moscow under Boris Yeltsin. A major collection of his poetry is in preparation now in Moscow.

Aleksey Shelvakh, born in 1948, worked for twenty-eight years as a lathe operator in Leningrad, now St. Petersburg. He has been an editor and translator (primarily of fantasy) for the publishers Azbuka and Amphora. His poems were originally published in samizdat, and now in a number of anthologies and magazines in Russia and the United States.

Sergey Magid, born in 1947 in Leningrad, has lived in Prague since 1990, and works in the Czech National Library. A mutual friend showed me, in typescript, his long poem "Paradise County Seat" in Leningrad in 1989. I copied it over laboriously by hand into my notebook, and later translated it. The punctuation and format in English follow the original Russian text.

Aleksandra Sozonova, born in 1956, is a St. Petersburg poet, screenwriter and novelist whom I met at the home of the friends who introduced me to Magid's poem, the theologian Grigory Benevich and his wife, also a talented poet, Olga Popova.

Nikolai Baitov was born in 1951 in Moscow, where he continues to live. "I always counted literature among the basic occupations of my life, but I never published anything, and for all practical purposes didn't even try until the political situation in our country (and with it the æsthetic climate) changed." One book of poems, *Ravnovesiia Raznoglasii* [*Equilibria of Disagreements*] was published in 1990, and another, *Vremena goda* [*Seasons*] in 2001.

Arsen Mirzaev, born in 1960 in Leningrad, was one of the founding editors of the journal *Sumerki* in 1989, and has published numerous essays, poems, articles and other writings in anthologies. He has published five collections of his own poems.

ACKNOWLEDGMENTS

Poems in this collection have previously been published in the following magazines and anthologies:

Æsop's Feast, Arion's Dolphin, Ars Interpres (Sweden), *Bluff City, Carve, The Chowder Review, Cumberlands, Cyphers* (Ireland), *Elixir, The Florida Review, Gargoyle, Kansas Quarterly, The Larcom Review, The Little Magazine, Long Pond Review, Lynx, The Massachusetts Review, Mid-American Review, New England Review, Oxford Magazine, Painted Bride Quarterly, The Prairie Star, Response, St. Petersburg Review, Slant, Stand* (United Kingdom), *Subtropics, Takahe* (New Zealand), *Thunder Mountain Review, Two Lines, The Washout Review, Writ* (Canada), *Zeugma, Bigger Than They Appear, The Blacksmith Anthology, Dear Winter, The Gospels in Our Image, Poems: A Celebration*

ABOUT THE AUTHOR

J. KATES is a poet, literary translator, and the president and co-director of Zephyr Press, a nonprofit press that focuses on contemporary works in translation from Russia, Eastern Europe and Asia. He received a National Endowment for the Arts Creative Writing Fellowship in Poetry in 1984 and a Translation Project Fellowship in 2006, as well as an Individual Artist Fellowship from the New Hampshire State Council on the Arts in 1995. He has published three chapbooks of his own poems: *Mappemonde* (Oyster River Press) *Metes and Bounds* (Accents Publishing) and *The Old Testament* (Cold Hub Press). He is the translator of *The Score of the Game* and *An Offshoot of Sense* by Tatiana Shcherbina; *Say Thank You* and *Level with Us* by Mikhail Aizenberg; *When a Poet Sees a Chestnut Tree* and *Secret Wars* by Jean-Pierre Rosnay; *Corinthian Copper* by Regina Derieva; and *Live by Fire* by Aleksey Porvin. He is the translation editor of *Contemporary Russian Poetry*, and the editor of *In the Grip of Strange Thoughts: Russian Poetry in a New Era.* A former president of the American Literary Translators Association, he is also the co-translator of four books of Latin American poetry.

THE HOBBLEBUSH GRANITE STATE
· POETRY SERIES

HOBBLEBUSH BOOKS *publishes several New Hampshire
poets each year, poets whose work has already received
recognition but deserves to be more widely known. The
editors are Sidney Hall Jr. and Rodger Martin.
For more information, visit the Hobblebush
website: www.hobblebush.com.*